★

FUN & CREATIVE
WORKSHOP ACTIVITIES

COOL
WOODWORKING
PROJECTS

REBECCA
FELIX

Checkerboard
Library

An Imprint of Abdo Publishing
abdopublishing.com

ABDOPUBLISHING.COM

Published by Abdo Publishing, a division of ABDO, PO Box 398166, Minneapolis, Minnesota 55439. Copyright © 2017 by Abdo Consulting Group, Inc. International copyrights reserved in all countries. No part of this book may be reproduced in any form without written permission from the publisher. Checkerboard Library™ is a trademark and logo of Abdo Publishing.

Printed in the United States of America, North Mankato, Minnesota
062016
092016

Design and Production: Mighty Media, Inc.
Series Editor: Paige V. Polinsky
Photo Credits: Rebecca Felix, Paige V. Polinsky, Shutterstock

The following manufacturers/names appearing in this book are trademarks: Black & Decker®, DeWALT®, Elmer's® Carpenter's® Wood Glue, Minwax®, Stanley®, Varathane®

Library of Congress Cataloging-in-Publication Data

Names: Felix, Rebecca, 1984- author.
Title: Cool woodworking projects : fun & creative workshop activities / Rebecca Felix.
Description: Minneapolis, Minnesota : Abdo Publishing, [2017] | Series: Cool industrial arts | Includes index.
Identifiers: LCCN 2016006308 (print) | LCCN 2016009211 (ebook) | ISBN 9781680781304 (print) | ISBN 9781680775501 (ebook)
Subjects: LCSH: Woodwork--Juvenile literature.
Classification: LCC TT185 .F45 2017 (print) | LCC TT185 (ebook) | DDC 684.08--dc23
LC record available at http://lccn.loc.gov/2016006308

TO ADULT HELPERS

This is your chance to help children learn about industrial arts! They will also develop new skills, gain confidence, and make cool things. These activities are designed to teach children how to work with wood. Readers may need more assistance for some activities than others. Be there to offer guidance when they need it. Encourage them to do as much as they can on their own. Be a cheerleader for their creativity!

Look at the beginning of each project for its difficulty rating (EASY, INTERMEDIATE, ADVANCED).

TABLE OF CONTENTS

WHAT

IS WOODWORKING?

Wood has been used for thousands of years to make millions of products. It is very **versatile**. Trees are processed into lumber which is used to build structures all around the world. Woodworkers cut, carve, saw, screw, and shape wood to create furniture, art, musical instruments, and more.

WOODWORKING TECHNIQUES

Workshop Tips

Setting up a safe workspace is important before beginning any woodworking project. It can be in the garage, in the basement, or at the kitchen table. Just make sure you get **permission**!

- Keep tools free of wood chips and dust. Make sure tools are kept off the floor and are unplugged when not in use.

- Work in a well-lit area.

- Wear closed-toe shoes in case you drop a sharp or heavy tool.

- Protect your eyes. Wear safety goggles *every* time you cut, drill, screw, or sand wood.

- Most importantly, *always be alert!* Keep fingers and hands away from blades and drill **bits**. Not paying attention could cost you a finger!

Essential Safety Gear

- Gloves

- Safety goggles

- Face mask

- Closed-toe shoes

Be Prepared

- Read the entire project before you begin.

- Make sure you have everything you need to do the project.

- Follow the directions carefully.

- Clean up after you are finished.

ADULT HELPERS

Working with wood can be **dangerous**. It often requires sharp saws and power tools. That means you should have an adult standing by for some of these projects.

KEY SYMBOLS

In this book, you may see one or more symbols at the beginning of a project. Here is what they mean:

SUPER SHARP!
A sharp tool is needed. Get help!

GLOVES
Hand protection should be worn for certain steps in this project.

HOT!
This project requires hot tools. Handle with caution.

SAFETY GOGGLES
Eye protection should be worn for certain steps in this project.

FACE MASK
Doing this project creates dust or requires glues with strong odors. A face mask should be worn for protection.

TOOLS OF THE TRADE

Here are some of the materials you will need for the projects in this book.

BINDER CLIPS

BOUNCY BALLS

COLORED PENCILS

COPING SAW

CRAFT FOAM

CRAFT STICKS

DOWELS

DRILL & DRILL BIT

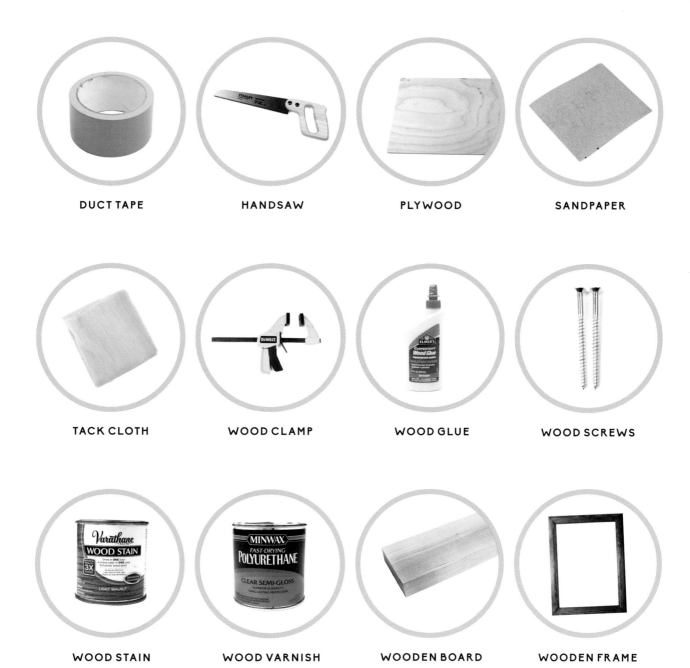

DUCT TAPE

HANDSAW

PLYWOOD

SANDPAPER

TACK CLOTH

WOOD CLAMP

WOOD GLUE

WOOD SCREWS

WOOD STAIN

WOOD VARNISH

WOODEN BOARD

WOODEN FRAME

MINI SKATEBOARD

MAKE A FINGER SKATEBOARD TO ROLL, JUMP, AND FLIP!

MATERIALS

- 4 craft sticks
- ruler
- pencil
- scissors
- sandpaper
- water
- glass
- 4 binder clips
- newspaper
- acrylic paint
- paintbrush
- duct tape
- 4 beads that fit on toothpicks
- 2 toothpicks
- hot glue gun & glue sticks

PREPPING + SOAKING

1 Measure and cut a craft stick to 3 inches (7.6 cm) long.

2 Clip the square corners off the craft stick and sand them round.

3 Soak the stick in a glass of water for 3 to 4 hours.

FORMING + CLAMPING

1 Carefully and gently bend the ends of the wet craft stick up.

Continued on the next page.

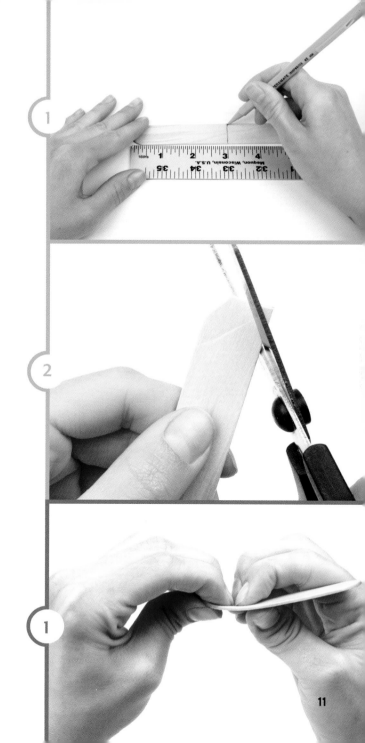

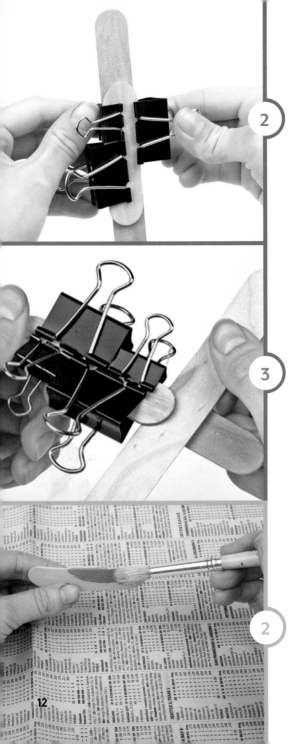

2 Secure the short craft stick to one long craft stick with binder clips. Make sure the bent ends you formed point up.

3 Wedge two craft sticks under each bent edge of the short craft stick. This will keep the ends turned up as the wood dries.

4 Keep the wedges and binder clips in place and let the wood dry for several hours, or overnight.

DECORATE

1 Remove the binder clips and wedges. The craft stick will have dried in the shape of a skateboard!

2 Cover your work surface with newspaper. Paint the skateboard. Use bright colors or make a design.

MAKING WHEELS + AXLES

1 Cut a thin strip of duct tape. Wrap it around a bead. Repeat for the other three beads.

2 Cut two toothpicks so they fit across the skateboard with a wheel on each side.

3 Put a small dot of hot glue on one end of each toothpick. Let it dry.

4 Thread two beads on each toothpick. Put a small dot of hot glue on the other end of the toothpicks. Let the glue dry.

5 Push the beads to the ends of the toothpicks. Glue the toothpicks to the bottom of the skateboard. Let the glue dry.

6 Use your fingers to move your super-small skateboard!

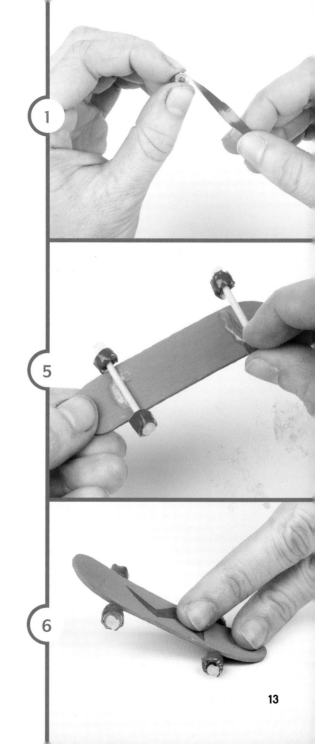

13

COLORED PENCIL ART + FRAME

SAW COLORED PENCILS TO CREATE 3-D FRAMES OR ART!

MATERIALS

- wooden frame, 4" × 6" (10 × 15 cm)
- newspaper
- acrylic paint
- paintbrush
- rubber bands
- 24 colored pencils
- wood clamp
- handsaw
- 60-grit sandpaper
- dry-erase marker
- super glue
- wood glue
- photo, printed design, or various art materials and paper

PREPPING THE FRAME

1 Take the glass and backing out of the frame.

2 Cover your work surface with newspaper. Paint the frame. Make it colorful! Let the paint dry.

CLAMPING + CUTTING

1 Rubber-band a few colored pencils together.

2 Clamp the ends of the colored pencils tightly to your workbench. The pencils should lie flat on the bench.

Continued on the next page.

3 Carefully cut the pencils with a handsaw. Cut halfway through the pencils with slow, long pulls toward you.

4 Then, use the tip of the saw blade to finish cutting through the pencils. Use short, fast pulls.

5 Keep sawing pieces off the pencils until you are near the clamp. Then unclamp and replace the pencils with new ones. Saw until all the pencils are in pieces. The pieces can be as short or as long as you like!

SANDING + GLUING

I   Some of the sawed pieces will have jagged, split, or uneven ends. Use the sandpaper to smooth and flatten these ends.

2   Do you want to create a design on the glass? Use a dry-erase marker to draw your design on the frame's glass. Then super glue the pencil pieces on top of the marker. Let it dry and put the glass back in the frame.

3   Would you rather decorate the frame? Use wood glue to attach the pencil pieces to the frame. Let the glue dry.

4   Put a photo, design, or drawing in the frame, along with the glass. You can also use a dry-erase marker to write notes on the glass!

BOUNCY-BALL PADDLE

CARVE A COOL PADDLE AND MAKE YOUR OWN BOUNCY-BALL GAME!

MATERIALS

- ¼"-thick (0.6 cm) piece of craft plywood, at least 6" × 12" (15 × 30 cm)
- ruler
- pencil & eraser
- 2 wood clamps
- handsaw
- 60-grit sandpaper
- drill & drill bit
- acrylic paint
- paintbrush
- decorative duct tape
- large rubber band
- small bouncy ball

DRAWING THE PADDLE

1 Measure and mark a 6-inch (15 cm) square on the plywood.

2 Make a mark 2¼ inches (5.5 cm) in from one corner of the square. Make a vertical mark. Repeat this step going in from the right corner. Make another mark.

3 Use the ruler to draw lines from the marks to the edge of the plywood. This is the paddle's handle. Erase the **horizontal** line at the top of the paddle.

Continued on the next page.

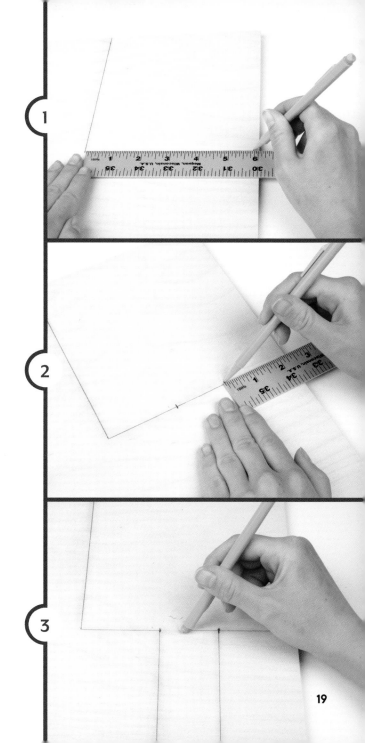

CUTTING THE PADDLE

1 Clamp the plywood to the workbench so the left side of the paddle hangs over the edge. Saw along the line.

2 Rotate and clamp the wood to cut the other lines. The line you are sawing should always be closest to the workbench.

3 Cut the handle so it is 4 inches (10 cm) long.

4 Sand the cut edges.

DRILLING HOLES

1 Make a mark 3 inches (7.5 cm) from one corner along the paddle's top edge. Then measure 3 inches (7.5 cm) down from the mark. Put your finger on this spot. Mark a dot on each side of your finger.

2 Clamp the paddle to the workbench with the marks hanging over the edge. Drill holes through each dot. Sand the holes if needed.

DECORATING + FINISHING

1 Paint the paddle. Let it dry.

2 Wrap the paddle's edges in duct tape. Wrap several layers of tape around the handle.

3 Cut the rubber band. Thread one end through both holes. Tie a knot to secure.

4 Wrap the other end of the rubber band around the ball and tie a knot. Then wrap the rubber band the opposite direction and tie again.

5 **Bounce** and dribble the ball on the board!

TIP

If you are having trouble bouncing the ball, your rubber band may be too long. Untie the rubber band at the board. Retie it to make it shorter.

21

PUT-IT-ON-DISPLAY
BOOKENDS

HOLD UP BOOKS AND
PUT YOUR FAVORITE
TOYS, TROPHIES, OR
PLANTS ON DISPLAY!

MATERIALS

- 2" × 4" (5.1 x 10.2 cm) piece of oak or cedar at least 4' (1.2 m) long
- ruler
- pencil
- 2 wood clamps
- handsaw
- 60-grit sandpaper
- tack cloth
- newspaper
- rubber gloves
- wood stain
- stir stick
- paintbrush
- old rag
- drill & drill bits
- 4 deck screws
- screwdriver or screw bit for the drill
- wood varnish
- large, long rubber band
- hot glue gun & glue sticks
- various display items: flowerpots, trophies, trinkets, or toys

MEASURING + CUTTING

1 Measure and mark 7.5 inches (19.1 cm) from the end of a piece of wood.

2 Clamp the wood to the workbench. Make sure the mark hangs over the edge.

3 Have an adult help you saw the wood along the line.

4 Repeat steps 1 through 3 with another piece of wood.

5 Measure, clamp, and cut two more pieces of wood. Make them each 4.5 inches (11.4 cm) long.

Continued on the next page.

SANDING + STAINING

1 You should now have two long and two short pieces of wood.

2 Clamp sandpaper to the workbench. Sand all uneven edges. Then use the sandpaper to smooth the entire surface of every piece.

3 Rub the sanded pieces with the tack cloth. This removes all dust.

4 Cover your work surface with newspaper. Put on gloves. Stir the wood stain. Paint it on the wood.

5 Rub the stained wood in the direction of the **grain** with the rag. Let the stain dry.

DRILLING + CONNECTING

1 Lay a long piece of wood down vertically with a wider side facing up. Mark ¾ inch (1.9 cm) up and in from both bottom corners.

2 Clamp a short piece to the long piece in an *L* shape. The two marks should be on the bottom edge facing out.

3 Clamp the *L* upside down to your workbench. Drill holes through the two marks.

4 Screw a wood screw into each drilled hole.

5 Repeat steps 1 through 4 with the other two pieces of wood.

SEALING + FINISHING

1 Paint a layer of wood varnish on the bookends. Let it dry.

2 Cut the rubber band into four even pieces. Hot glue two pieces along the bottom of each bookend. Let the glue dry. Neatly store books and more using your new bookends!

BENDING BOW + DOWEL ARROWS

BEND A WOODEN BOW AND SEND WOODEN ARROWS FLYING!

MATERIALS

- ruler
- 1/8" (0.3 cm) craft plywood, 12" × 24" (30 × 61 cm), thick
- pencil
- wood clamps
- handsaw
- scrap wood
- drill & drill bit
- 60-grit sandpaper
- bathtub
- water
- box, 17.5" × 11.5" × 8" (44.5 × 29.2 × 20.3 cm)
- 2 to 4 dowels, 12" × ¼" (30 × 0.6 cm)
- coping saw
- newspaper
- acrylic paint
- paintbrush
- scissors
- craft foam
- hot glue gun & glue sticks
- duct tape
- large, long rubber band

MAKING THE BOW

1 Measure a strip of plywood 2 by 24 inches (5 by 61 cm).

2 Clamp the plywood to the workbench. Cut along the lines with the handsaw. Use the tip of the saw. Make small, steady pulls until you have cut out the strip.

3 Mark a dot near each end of the strip.

4 Clamp the strip to the workbench with scrap wood beneath it. Drill a hole through each mark.

Continued on the next page.

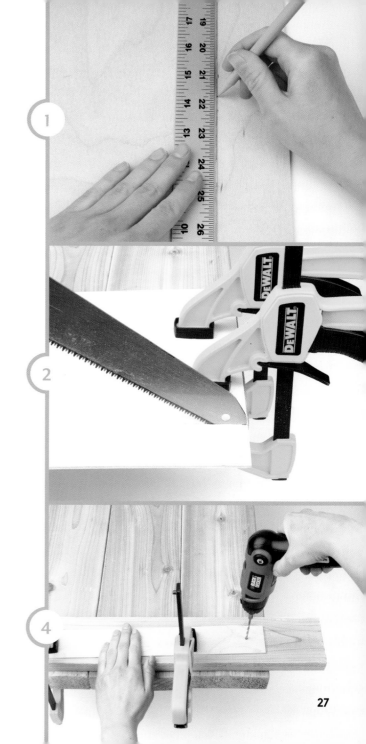

27

5 Sand all rough edges of the strip and the drilled holes.

BENDING + DRYING THE BOW

1 Fill a bathtub with a few inches of water. Soak the strip for at least 12 hours.

2 Remove the strip from the water. Carefully bend it into an arch. Slowly bend and **flex** small sections at a time. Repeat until the entire strip is **pliable**.

3 Lay the strip in the box. Place it on its side so the ends press against the box sides and the curve keeps its shape. Let the strip dry for 12 hours. This is your bow.

MAKING ARROWS

1 Clamp a **dowel** to the workbench. Use the coping saw to cut a notch in one end. Repeat for all dowels.

2 Cover your work surface with newspaper. Paint the dowels. Let the paint dry.

3 Cut small triangles out of craft foam. Glue two triangles to the unnotched end of each dowel. These are your arrowheads.

PAINTING + STRINGING

1 Remove the bow from the box. Paint it and let the paint dry.

Continued on the next page.

29

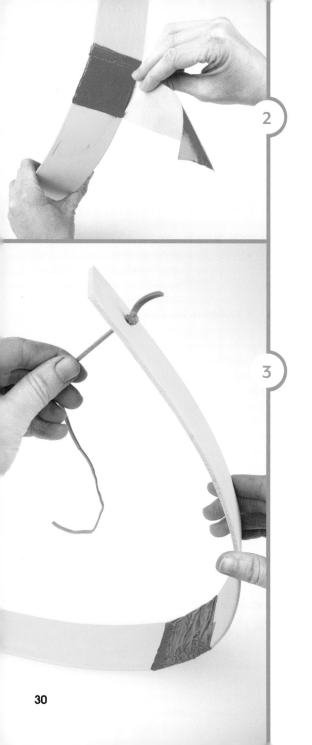

2 Wrap several layers of duct tape around the bow's center. This makes a padded handle.

3 Cut the rubber band. Thread one end of the rubber band through a hole in the bow. Tie the end in a knot on the outside of the bow. Attach the other end of the rubber band to the other end of the bow.

4 Take your bow and arrows outside. Hold the bow and place a notched **dowel** on the rubber band. Pull back, and aim it away from any people. See how far your arrow will fly!

TIP
If the rubber band is not tight enough, carefully pull and wrap it around the width of the bow a couple of times.

GLOSSARY

BIT – a replaceable part of a drill that makes holes or screws in screws.

BOUNCE – to cause something to hit a surface so it springs back.

DANGEROUS – able or likely to cause harm or injury.

DOWEL – a round rod or stick.

FLEX – to bend or stretch something.

GRAIN – the way the lines or fibers in something, such as wood, are arranged.

HORIZONTAL – going side to side, parallel to the ground.

PERMISSION – when a person in charge says it's okay to do something.

PLIABLE – able to bend easily.

VERSATILE – having many uses.

Websites

To learn more about Cool Industrial Arts, visit **booklinks.abdopublishing.com**. These links are routinely monitored and updated to provide the most current information available.

INDEX